CU00842869

The Reinvention Method

8 Steps to transform your life…

EVEN if you have found it impossible in the past

Avril Gill

All Rights Reserved.

Copyright © Avril Gill

No part of this book may be reproduced or transmitted in any form or by any means, electrical or mechanical, including photocopying and recording, or by any information storage or retrieval system without permission in writing from the author.

Disclaimer:

This book is written for informational purposes only. The author has made every effort to make sure the information is complete and accurate. All attempts have been made to verify information at the time of this publication and the author does not assume any responsibility for errors, omissions, or other interpretations of the subject matter.

The publisher and author shall have neither liability nor responsibility to any person or entity with respect to any loss or damage caused or alleged to be caused directly or indirectly by this book.

Table of Contents

Reviews

"Here is an engaging, pragmatic ode to living... taking responsibility for one's own life! So refreshing, clear, inviting and peppered with the author's personal narrative.

After reading Avril's book, I feel the joy and lightness she describes and am inspired to pay greater attention to my thoughts and beliefs so I can truly take charge of my life.

I will be sending this book out to others this Christmas."

Nicola MacKenzie
Craniosacral & Yoga Therapist & Teacher

"Are you ready to own your story and become the author of the next chapter in your life? If the answer is yes, then this is the book for you.

The Reinvention Method provides a unique 8-Step approach to really recognize and discover what it is that's really stopping you from leading the life you want, or maybe even one that you never imagined possible.

Written with fearless honesty, Avril blends her own personal journey with her many years experience as an established coach, teacher and therapist. I would highly recommend for anyone who wants to transform their lives and become the very best version of themselves."

Lynne Sutherland
LMS Hypnotherapy & Coaching

"The book is a practical 8 step guide to making positive changes in your life. It is easy to follow and you need no previous knowledge or experience to understand and implement these steps.

I loved how practical the steps are, they are a no nonsense approach to making changes and explain why each step is important so you cannot quickly gloss over and choose only the easy steps to do, you understand the connection with each step and how it relates to the bigger process of change.

I like that the process is easily broken down for me to go through and puts the responsibility and actions on me to make the change! It's a practical process that isn't about manifesting or simply having a positive mind-set, it's what you actually do to get what you actually want. The steps can be applied to almost any area of your life where you want change.

Great book, I recommend it for anyone who wants a practical guide to making changes and that are willing to take the action to make it happen.

Orielle Taylor
Hypnotherapy Coach & Trainer

"So much of your book resonated with me. I feel like you have handed me something that has just switched something on in my brain. I know change is down to me. I know for change to happen I have to work on it and take inspired action. I know I am more than I allow myself to believe and I love the almost shamanic aspect of our shadow self. I also have never 'got' the gratitude journal. Writing I'm grateful for the roof over my head, my kids, blah, blah, blah never really evoked any true feeling in me. But spending time with Seth and seeing his wee face light up at simple things gives me that feeling of deep joy and love for just being with him in that moment.

You have put everything together, simply and how it is. I feel empowered today to take charge and be the change I want to see. I've wallowed too long and want to start living the life I deserve! Because I do bloody deserve it!!

Anyway, I'm going back to chapter one and note taking!!!

Thank you Avril, this has given me an excitement today that I can transform - watch this space!! No more limiting beliefs!

Laura Beth Clark
Business Owner/Mompreuneur

"This book is a powerful testament to Avril's ability to deliver profound insights for transformation, into a clear and digestible blueprint for action. The Reinvention Method is a down to earth, practical and hugely empowering guide to taking back the reigns of your life - today!'

Caitlin MacKenzie
Holistic Coach

Acknowledgements

This book would not have been possible without the support, guidance and inspiration of so many people. I always remember my Nana saying to me "don't die with the book still in you Avril, no matter how little you think of what you have to say there will be a world of people out there waiting and needing to hear your words." I believe that to be true now, and I thank her each and every day for being a guiding light in my early childhood years and wish she was here today to read the words I write on a daily basis. Without her and her words that have lived inside my head all my life, I would never have had the courage to write this or any other book.

There are so many people I want to thank for helping me, and way more than I could possibly acknowledge her, including those who have a place in back in my distant memories and while often not with me in my daily thoughts, their influence and teachings continue to linger in my life today. I would, however, like to publicly show my appreciation and give thanks to the following people who have helped me in so many different ways:

Orielle Taylor, my dear friend and business associate who never ceases to amaze and surprise me, her stamina and staying power, is incredible and her loyalty and commitment to me and the work we do together are inspiring. Thank you, my dear friend.

Annette Philip, my personal assistant and dear friend, for keeping me organised, cheering me on and reading my drafts, and just for being there for me at all the right times.

My husband Alan, who never expects anything from me and without even being aware, is a living walking and talking example of what I teach and write about on a daily basis. A natural at living life compassionately with no need to attach any labels to it, a true spiritual warrior. My deepest love and appreciation for the strong roots you bring to my life and the lives of our girls. I am blessed to share my life with you.

My family who are my greatest teachers.

To the entire Transformation Summit team, the community and everyone else involved, thank you for creating this opportunity I am so glad I decided to reinvent me from teacher and coach to author and jump on board with your community.

And most especially to my daughters Alison and Ara, just in case I haven't told you today, I love you. You are my greatest gift and I am truly blessed to share my life with you both.

The Reinvention Method – 8 steps to reinvent yourself and transform your life…Even if you have found it impossible in the past.

"There's no use trying", said Alice, "one can't' believe in impossible things.' "I daresay you haven't had much practice," said the Queen. "When I was your age I used to practice for half an hour a day. Why sometimes I've even believed as many as six impossible things before breakfast."

-Lewis Carrol,
Alice in Wonderland

To Mum & Dad

Because of you, I learned it was ok to "just be me".

I love you and miss you both.

Introduction

It might seem like a big bold statement to say that you can reinvent yourself any time you want, and you may not think it's possible. Like many people, maybe you are thinking, but how can anyone possibly make a decision just to change who they are?

Well, I am here to share with you how easy it is and how you can quite literally reinvent yourself anytime you wish. Because that's exactly what I have been doing for the last ten years of my life and I am going to take you through the steps I use to do just that and have used to help hundreds of my clients completely transform their life.

Before we do that, though, I want to share a little bit about me with you. It's important that you get that I am not another one of these coaches or teachers who decided to become a coach because it seemed like a nice thing to do, or because I went on a coaching course or attended a life coaching seminar. I do this because of my own lived personal experience and because I know what I teach can and does change people's lives, just as it has changed mine.

My life didn't start easily; I had a traumatic childhood tainted with abuse and all sorts of stuff that according to many professional psychologists should have hindered my chances of having a happy and prosperous life. And to be honest for the first half of my life they were right! I was so messed up because of my childhood I struggled to live a happy life, have meaningful relationships with people or enjoy life to the full.

I was literally at war with myself, even though by the time I hit my thirties I had a successful marriage and career behind me and everything that from the outside looking in should mean I was happy, fulfilled and complete.

But I wasn't, inside my life was a mess, not a day would go by when I didn't like myself and found ways to corrupt anything good that came along. I was cynical, resentful, jealous and just downright miserable. My moods swung from being deliriously happy to desperately depressed and full of anger or rage. I tried everything to help myself. I went for counseling and spent years reading all different types of self-help books, from basic psychology to the more esoteric or spiritual. Connecting with guides and angels to past life regression, you name it by the time I was thirty I had tried everything. I just wanted to see if it made any difference to how I felt about me. I even did an honours degree in psychology! Nothing seemed to change how I felt; I still felt unhappy!

I remember I went to a "healer" who claimed that they could download information and help me heal my ancestral DNA and work with lots of past life issues which apparently was the reason I felt the way I felt. So for months I had early morning regression sessions and listened to audios and read books, hoping and praying that this would change how I felt inside.

And it did to be honest, for a while I would feel different, life did improve a little, and I seemed a bit happier, but it would soon pass.

Nothing I did seemed to last, however; no amount of crystals, angels, or any other kind of healing or therapy worked for me. I kept on searching for something because I was desperate to get rid of this unhappiness I felt deep down inside and some of the behaviours I had because of how unhappy I was. I was fed up getting myself into debt just to feel good for a short time; I was fed up going out with people I didn't enjoy being around just so as I could feel liked by others because I didn't like myself. I was so fed up with doing things that I thought would make me happy yet deep inside I still felt as miserable as I did when I was a child. In fact, the further I got into my thirties the sadder and unhappy I became and this affected everything and everyone around me.

The turning point for me happened a couple of years before my 40th birthday. I remember I had just turned 38 and the organisation I was working for was going through some major changes, I was given a big promotion and instead of being happy I felt like my life was over. I looked back on my career with this organisation and thought this is it, even with this promotion I still didn't believe I was good enough. I thought to myself what is the point of all of this when I am still so unhappy with my life? I had worked hard, striving to leave behind a childhood of poverty and abuse only to get here and still feel no different inside to when I left home at fifteen. I had had enough and was ready to walk away from my career, my marriage, and my daughter.

It was then that I realised that no matter what I did on the outside I was never going to feel different, and I realised that I needed to change me on the inside, but I had tried everything and didn't know what to do or how to make these changes last. And it just hit me, from nowhere. After years of reading all sorts of self-help and personal development books I suddenly got it, if I could just change what I believed about me, Avril and create a whole new me, a new set of beliefs about me, I could reinvent myself from the inside out.

And that was what I did, I stripped out all these old beliefs I had about myself and my life and saw them for the lies that they were and began piece by piece completely reinventing the person I wanted to become. I stopped listening and reading all that esoteric stuff about past lives and it being part of my DNA and I began to focus on the here and now. What was right in front of me and what specifically I could do that would give me a different result. I stopped searching and started taking action to make powerful and real changes for me on the inside.

Because I realised that I wasn't born with the beliefs I had about myself, no! All of those beliefs, lies and anything else I was carrying that made me unhappy were a bi-product of some outside influence that I had taken on to be true for me. These were just thoughts, thoughts that I thought on for long enough that they became beliefs. And if I had acquired them, then surely I can change them or delete them and create a whole new of set beliefs, or a whole new set of thoughts to think on until they became new beliefs. In fact, why not create a whole new me through my thoughts and beliefs!

That's what I did, I set about Reinventing myself and transforming my life, and what's more, it didn't take me another ten years of reading self-help books or going to so-called healing gurus', no, I decided to change overnight. In a matter of weeks and with a little help from a fantastic coach and mentor I reinvented my whole outlook and transformed every aspect of my life, my career, my marriage and all my relationships. I stopped being passive and started being the person I wanted to be.

Life is a constant process of reinventing who you are, those who have created a happy, successful life for themselves know this. Many people however never come to the realisation that they can actually reinvent themselves at any time. Most people need a crisis in their life to do this, I was once that person after each life crisis happened I struggled through and somehow unconsciously managed to reinvent myself to create a new way of living so I no longer felt the pain of my life crisis.

There was my crisis after spending 10 years "trying" for a baby unsuccessfully, there was a crisis in my career, several crises with my finances, a crisis with my marriage, a crisis with family relationships and after the death of my mum, well that was a major life meltdown for me. And there have been many, many more, what I have realised is that I have unconsciously reinvented myself for me to survive and come out the other end.

What I have learned through all of this is that I do not have to wait for the crisis to unconsciously reinvent myself I can consciously do this anytime I want. In fact, if I choose I can become someone different right here and now at this moment and all it takes is for me to consciously drop the stories and any victim mindset that is keeping me as the person I am and consciously choose a new story and begin being who I want to be.

It's been such a liberating and empowering realisation to embody, and it has enabled me to shift my life from a place of striving to be able to thrive. Reinventing yourself happens in a place of peace, not when you are frantically trying to run your life, it starts in the centre of your being, a silent decision is made and a commitment and a new you is created!

Fast forward another ten years and I am now sharing my story. Coaching and teaching others to do the same and transform their life and in this book, I am going share with you what I have come to realise are the eight key steps that I took in those weeks that actually turned my life around and what I continue to use anytime I want to reinvent myself.

If you have had enough and have wanted to transform your life, but have struggled to do so, you can start today by using this book to help you to reinvent yourself and become the person you have always wanted to become! It's straightforward, no-nonsense steps for a change and if used and followed your life will change too!

Chapter one

"Freedom is not the absence of commitments, but the ability to choose - and commit myself to - what is best for me."

-Paulo Coelho, The Zahir

Step 1 – Making the commitment to change

"There's no scarcity of opportunity to make a living at what you love. There is only a scarcity of resolve to make it happen."

- Wayne W. Dyer

So many people spend their life saying if only things could be different or if I didn't do this or have that problem or this responsibility then I could enjoy my life. So few realise that for anything to change they have got to want to change. I have worked with hundreds of clients who have come to me wanting to change aspects of their life, yet, like me all those years back were not fully committed to making change happen.

In fact, so many clients come along hoping that I will be able to change them, just as I did in the past, each time I read a new book or met another so called guru. I believed they would be the one with the secret ingredient that would tell me exactly how to change and would help me do it. I, like many of my clients who seek me out for help, was so passive, not realising that if you really wanted to change, you needed to be committed to making changes. Not just making changes for the few hour's it takes to read a book or the short time spent listening to a counsellor or coach, or the few days listening to a guru at a seminar. But full out committed in the long run to change. It takes real effort every day and every way to actively engage in the process of changing who you believe yourself to be.

You have got to go full out to change, that's why so many self-help programs fail not because they aren't any good but because the people who attend or use them are only half committed to making changes. They like the idea of change but don't like the effort it takes, and like anything that's worth anything, it takes effort, practice and commitment change.

I'm a trained hypnotherapist, and I teach people to become hypnotherapists and what I have found most astonishing in my ten-year career as a hypnotherapist (and over 20 years as a coach); is the amount of people who come to me believing that I can change them at an unconscious level. All while they sit there in the chair with no effort or engagement on their part, and that they will leave my office a different person!

While I would suggest that there is an element of truth in the above, that some form of change may in fact occur but it will not happen without their commitment to change. For a change to happen it must involve deliberate action. Where you actively take charge of the things you want to change. No amount of me saying to you, "You will be confident" will EVER make you a confident person. The only thing that will make you confident is for you to go out and consciously and deliberately do the very things you want to be confident in, which in turn will create positive experiences that can be reinforced over time, all of which leads to confidence. I've never met a new driver, who feels confident after passing their driving test, but I have met people who have driven for fifteen years, who once lacked confidence but are super confident drivers now. Nobody gave them that confidence, they acquired that through practice and repeated experiences and a commitment to driving.

A client I had been working with for several months kept coming to sessions and complaining that their life still wasn't changing even though they said they worked through all things I share here in this book; still, my client never felt they had experienced any change. They were caught up in a cycle of negative thinking and negative self-talk and continuing to engage in harmful activities, and I said to them one day, you know I don't think I am the right coach for you, and maybe you should consider working with someone else. They were shocked and asked why and then I told them that I didn't believe they were committed to actually making the changes to their life, and if they are not committed then I am wasting their time and money.

At first, they were a bit shocked and after quite a long time of silence they turned to me and said you are right. I haven't been committed, I've been coming here, and we have worked through lots of things, but I haven't actually gone away and implemented anything, I just revert back to the old ways of being. And when I asked what was stopping them, they said because it was too much effort to be consciously aware and in the moment all the time. Bingo and there was the truth! It was easier for them to stay the same than to make a commitment to change. It was easier to live life asleep than to live it consciously aware in every moment being the navigator of their thoughts and destiny. It was easier to sleep through life and only take action when they felt good, or they had a good feeling about something or their horoscope suggested there were auspicious transits in their chart!

But here's the thing, you need to be committed during the difficult times, you need to be committed even when you do not feel good. You need to be consciously aware in every moment of how committed you are to changing your life, nothing less will do.

Because that's how change works, you must be committed, practice and create repeated experiences for yourself that reinforce the changes you are choosing to make in your life, regardless of what your horoscope says or how you feel!

I would suggest if this scares you, this idea of being full out committed to changing your life then maybe you are not ready, and you should stop reading now. And if it doesn't and you are ready to play full out in your own life then I dare you to make a commitment or a vow to yourself right here and now and fully commit to reinventing the person you are now and becoming the best version of you. It's the first step and the most important step. If you are only half committed then, you will only experience half the results, if any at all.

There are no fancy techniques, or super complicated rituals to reinventing your life, it really is simple, and if there is some sort of secret key or ingredient, then I would suggest it resides on your level of commitment and how committed you are to making the changes.

You have to know your path when it opens up to you, don't blow an opportunity because you are too blind or scared to take a risk or fear not knowing how things will work out.

Don't blow an opportunity because you can't be bothered to put the work in or make it happen or because it just feels like too much effort or it doesn't feel right. Don't blow an opportunity because it's not guaranteed to make you a success overnight or a superstar.

Sooner or later everyone has to find their courage and be brave enough to impose their self on life or settle themselves to a life of mediocrity or insignificance.

You are the only one that can make anything happen, don't be a victim and blame someone else or expect anyone else to do it for you. When you are less than satisfied with your life, with your business and the results you are getting ask yourself this; where in my life did I resign and decide to settle for mediocre? If you are brave enough, to be honest with yourself, you will find the answer to transforming your life."

Take that first step now and make a commitment to yourself, to your life, and to the person you know you are.

Chapter Two

"Closing cycles. Not because of pride, incapacity or arrogance, but simply because that no longer fits your life. Shut the door, change the record, clean the house, shake off the dust. Stop being who you were, and change into who you are."

- Paulo Coelho

Step 2 - Let go of the past now!

"Renew, release, let go. Yesterday's gone. There's nothing you can do to bring it back. You can't "should've" done something. You can only DO something. Renew yourself. Release that attachment. Today is a new day!"

— Steve Maraboli

Yes, I know you've heard that one before and so had I, so many times! From friends, family, and therapists, but somehow I couldn't let go of the grip I had on my past. It was like an old friend I had outgrown but couldn't quite live without. I knew it served me no purpose to keep going back over the past and the things that had happened to me or the mistakes I had made. Yet for some reason, it was like a tumour, and just when I would think I had finally got rid of it, something would happen in my life and trigger an old feeling that was connected to something from my past. And that would be me, I would fall all the way back down the hole again, like Alice in Wonderland falling down that rabbit hole unable to catch hold of anything to stop me from falling, I just went tumbling down into the world full of confusion again. Tainted with memories from the past and stories I would tell myself about all reasons that I was really a fake and a failure.

I'd let thoughts and memories take over, I would spend days thinking about all the stuff that had happened to me and how unfair it was and how other people didn't understand. And the longer I stayed there, the more powerfully the past took hold of me. Old feelings of anger and resentment would bubble up, relationships would be affected, and sometimes I would hide out for weeks and days and completely disconnect myself from people because I felt so sorry for myself and because they didn't understand me. No amount of me attempting to get them to understand though would ever change anything, and I tried, and this would add to my misery over the past. I just didn't get why they didn't understand that my awful past had made me so desperately unhappy, and how could they be happy when someone they loved was so miserable.

I remember my father once saying to me, "Avril you have got to let go of the past." And I remember feeling so angry at him for not understanding why it was so important for him to acknowledge everything that I had been through, and why I couldn't let it go, it just wasn't that easy!

After spending so much time and money working on myself and my past and getting nowhere, in fact sometimes getting deeper and deeper into the drama of my past that I couldn't move forward in life I became so sick of my past, I decided to just let it go. At that moment I suddenly realised that it was simple. It was a simple conscious choice that I could make each and every day, to choose to go there or to decide to go somewhere else. I realised that what was actually going on in my mind was a replay of old stories and events that were no longer real for me. And at that moment I made another commitment, I committed to never again choosing my past over what was happening in my life now or over my future. I vowed to not spend one more minute in wasted energy ruminating over all the hurt or pain I had experienced in my life or caused others.

I literally let it go, and anytime those old thoughts or feelings raised their ugly faces, in my mind, I made a conscious choice to take my focus elsewhere and reminded myself that these were no longer real, only images in my mind about a time that no longer exists. The past is not real, it's not happening now, the only thing that makes it real is your thinking about it at this moment. When you are not thinking about it does not exist.

Anytime I was reminded of how I had been wronged or hurt, I would ask myself is this real and does this serve me right now to go there?

Always the answer would be no, so I made that commitment not to go there and focus on something different, anything even if it was just hanging out the washing!

I stopped analysing the why of the past or figuring out what this person or that person was teaching me and accepted that these were experiences I had and at any time I could consciously to choose to create new experiences for myself. But while focusing on those old past events, I was stopping myself engaging in my life at the moment now.

You see part of the problem that everyone faces when making changes in their life is that they get stuck in the past and come up with all sorts of reasons and excuses about why they cannot change. Believing that their past experiences are what determines the outcomes they experience in their life right now. And to some extent, they are right, but only in that they choose to believe that they are still the same person they were, say five, two or even one year ago. And that just isn't true!

That's a lie we tell our self. We are not the same person we were yesterday, let alone a year ago. Yet we continue to believe we are because we hold on to old perceptions, past experiences and old beliefs. Because these early experiences and ideas about who we are, are like old friends, we have outgrown. We just don't know how to drop them and when we do people say to us "Oh you've changed" or "who do you think you are". And we start to doubt these new ideas or changes we want to make and revert back, back to our old ways, our old beliefs and behaviours, back to who or what we believed we were in the past.

But you have to make a choice, decide that this person you are today isn't the person you want to be, then commit to letting go of anything that gets in your way of living your best life.

You must let your past die for you to be born again bringing with you all the best parts of you into the future, and you need to be clear about just what it is you are letting go off.

Religions have been doing this for centuries, people get baptised and are born again free from the sins or ties of their past and free to rewrite the scripture of their new life, as reinvented people. If other people can do it, you can too. Anyone can do this, you simply make a conscious decision to let your past go and live here and now in this present moment focusing on what you have in your life and what you want to create.

Many of my clients have said to me that it's impossible for them to let go of the past because they have had so many awful things happen to them and I completely understand that. They don't believe me that it's easy, but after I tell them what I have been through, my struggles of overcoming sexual abuse in childhood, violence and poverty. Of being rejected by people who you would expect to love you and start to show them how easy it can be they too realise they can let go of the past and begin to experience lasting changes in their life.

One of my clients, I will call her Lucy spent 5 years in a marriage that was manipulative and struggled to trust people and every time she got close to someone she would cause the relationship to break up. Lucy believed that she would end up back in the same situation again and would rather be on her own than go through the experiences she had in the past. Yet there was a huge conflict for her, she didn't want to end up "old and alone" as she put it.

When we talked about the hold she had on her past, she insisted that it was important for her to remember the damage that relationship caused so as to ensure it never happened again. And I suggested that by keeping hold of those past experiences and not letting them go she wasn't protecting herself but that, she was preventing herself from ever experiencing a healthy relationship in the future and almost guaranteeing that she would end up "old and alone".

When she realised that she could still look after herself without the need to hold on to all that anger and fear from the past and let go of being a victim, Lucy was able to free herself and begin to reinvent her life and have the deep loving relationships that she actually wanted to experience. But as long as she kept hold of the past, she would continue to be someone who was filled with anger, resentment and therefore destroying any chance of having what she really wanted deep down inside.

By letting go of the past she was able to fully step into the person she wanted to be and the relationship, she wanted to create. Lucy learned how to reinvent her life, by making commitments to change and consciously choosing to create the life she wanted in the here and now.

The past doesn't take hold of us, we take hold of the past, and it's us who choose to cling to the past, not the other way around. The only reason the past continues to influence our life for good or ill is that we consciously choose to hold on to it.

To let go of the past, it's important to learn to accept it for what it was. Forgiving any wrongdoing, perceived or otherwise that was done to us or by us and really let it go by making peace with it. It's like saying goodbye to an old, worn out pair of shoes you have got used to wearing. Even though they are all tattered and worn and out of fashion, once they have gone and you get some new ones you slowly begin to break them in so they start to take on the shape and feel of your foot. And in no time at all the new shoes look and feel more glamorous than the old and are a much better fit for you.

Chapter Three

"If you spend your time hoping someone will suffer the consequences for what they did to your heart, then you're allowing them to hurt you a second time in your mind."

- Shannon L. Alder

Step 3 – Cultivate Acceptance and Forgiveness

It's important to really let go for us to move forward, and often people think they have moved on from a situation or bad experience or even a mistake they have made but still feel stuck even after they have forgiven a person for the wrong-doing or perceived wrong-doing. This is often why letting go of the past is so painful, we get stuck in a place of forgiveness.

Most people, including myself, get caught up in the idea that forgiveness will in and of itself release us from the hold that past hurts or past mistakes have had on us. We are taught this from an early age, often people say, "let's forgive and forget" or "forgive and move on". But that never actually happens, the forgiver still holds residual feelings of the event, and even if it's, you who have committed the crime, and you have worked hard to forgive yourself, deep down inside you still carry feelings of guilt. Believe me, I know, I have hurt many people in the past and have spent just as much time working on forgiving myself as forgiving others.

Now I am not saying that forgiveness isn't necessary, of course, it is, it's part of the process of letting in go, but to forgive we must fully understand that there is a much deeper level of forgiveness that we need to figure out before moving into a place of genuine forgiveness.

I have come to realise that there is so much more to forgiveness than we fully recognise. In fact, the very act of forgiveness instead of releasing us from the power of the wrongdoer does nothing other than shifting the power dynamics of the situation from them to you. And whether you consciously realise this or not, when you say you forgive someone either to yourself or to others you now have a hold over the person who has wronged you.

You see forgiveness is all about power, there is no equality in forgiveness, someone continues to own the balance of power and someone will always end up being in the wrong.

And so long as we hold on to this idea that we have done something wrong or have been wronged we can never truly let go of the past mistakes or the wrong doings experienced by us from other people. And deep down at an unconscious level, we will continue to harbour negative feelings, even if we are not consciously aware of them.

I have really grappled over the years with the process of forgiveness, especially as a result of coming to terms with my early childhood of abuse, and while saying I forgave the person it allowed me to take back a level of power but never fully allowed me to let go of that old experience.

I like many of my clients have spent time working through forgiveness, yet never fully releasing the hurt or guilt of those past negative experiences. What I have come to realise through my work and working with my clients is that to forgive we must first accept the individuals who have hurt us or wholly accept ourselves, as human beings, because, without acceptance, we can never truly forgive and let go.

Acceptance is a very different experience to forgiveness, and many would say to accept a situation or experience that is negative means to tolerate the situation or behaviour. That is not so. Acceptance I have come to experience is more about taking a higher ground, it's not about a shifting of the power dynamics within your relationship it's about learning to understand where the other person is coming from and why they behave the way the do.

It was only in my later years that I was able to genuinely forgive my parents, not because I had chosen to forgive them but because I began to accept them as they were. I began to understand that the actions they took or were taking were simply as a result of them doing the best they knew how. I realised that they didn't act in certain ways with the intent to cause me pain or harm in childhood or at any other time, they behaved in these ways because that was all they knew to do or all they could do to live their life at the moment.

As they and I grew older finding the space for acceptance was so much easier for me, and with that forgiveness became effortless, it wasn't something I had to actively do, it was something that just happened naturally as a result of me accepting them for who they were.

There is always a positive intention behind every behaviour, no matter how harmful that may on the surface appear. When you can learn to look into the shadows of the other person and begin to understand what that positive intention is, it's far easier to move into a place of acceptance. And when you can look into your own shadows and welcome them and accept them as part of who you are, a genuine transformation occurs.

Through the act of acceptance, I actually believe that you completely release the person from the wrongdoing, or release yourself from the wrongdoing. The person who has hurt or harmed you has no power over you, and you hold no power over them. Forgiveness then becomes a gentle, effortless and natural process. Not a forced process that one must do to let go of the past.

It does not mean you condone the behaviour or encourage it or like it, it just means you accept the person for who they are and understand why or what may have caused them to respond to life in that way.

Chapter Four

"Nothing binds you except your thoughts; nothing limits you except your fear, and nothing controls you except your beliefs."

- Marianne Williamson

Step 4 - Stop believing all the stuff you have been telling yourself

"Your thoughts and beliefs are not who you are, they are who your mind is."

Every time I work with a new client, it never ceases to amaze me the stories I hear them telling me about themselves, usually all negatively framed around how or why they are the way the are and why they are stuck in the situations they find themselves in.

Most of these stories they have about themselves they have been carrying since childhood. Often a client will say to me oh I'm not very creative, and I will ask how do you know that. They will then go on to tell me some story about their childhood and how their teacher or parents used to say to them that their skills lay somewhere else, or they were not good with their imagination. So they grow up believing that they are not creative, one client then went on to tell me about an affair he had been having for the last 5 years and shared all the very creative ways they have been hiding it from their partner! So who's not creative after all...Creativity takes on many, many different forms.

The beliefs we hold and the stories we believe about whom we are what make us. We literally create our personalities and character out of these beliefs and the stories we repeat about who we think we are throughout our life.

What's even more frightening is that most of these beliefs and stories that we own were mostly in the first instance made up for us, by someone else!

So when people say to me it's impossible to reinvent yourself; I quickly respond and remind them that if you don't reinvent yourself someone else will come along and invent a person for you to be. After all, our parents, friends, teachers and many others have been designing us on our behalf for years. So to take hold of our stories and start changing them before someone else does it for us is a bit of a no brainer really!

Be clear and be genuinely honest with yourself about where you are with positive empowering beliefs you have about, relationships, achievement, money and about your past, being happy, being successful, being free, being abundant, being and doing whatever it is you want to do.

Most people are so used to being stuck in their own story that they are not even aware of what that story is actually creating in their life, let alone the feelings it leaves them with. If you have a story about being a failure at something, whether that's in your career or relationships then that's its exactly what you are likely to keep creating for yourself.

My six-year-old daughter came home from school upset because she kept making mistakes with her maths and getting her sums wrong. Now I could easily have said don't worry pet, keep practising, and you will eventually become good at maths. Instead, I decided I wanted her to create a positive and empowering story about how beneficial it was to get things wrong, make mistakes and fail because I know the importance of the imprints of these types of beliefs have on us at this very early age.

So I said to her that's fantastic, isn't it wonderful that you know how to get things wrong, and every time you get something wrong you get the chance to find a different way of doing it, how lucky are you! Now she comes home and tells me all about the things she got wrong and how excited she is because she is going to find lots of new and different ways to fix her mistakes. You see children are born creators, they love making things up, inventing new things and working things out, it's adults who come along and change the story and their beliefs about how creative they are by insisting mistakes are wrong, and they need to get it right.

Begin to be consciously aware of the stories or beliefs you tell yourself, as you think about these things, are the feelings and thoughts empowering? Do you feel really great and believe nothing holds you back? Or, is there a niggling doubt, or a little voice in your head making you feel otherwise? Actually, listen, begin to connect with any belief/s or stories about yourself that you sense or are critical to holding you back in life or stopping you being the person you know you are. You most likely know what your limiting beliefs are, if not I have created a list of common ones in the appendix that may trigger yours.

Some years back a client came to me for help with their business. I had known this client from my old HR corporate days, and they knew I was pretty good at coming up with ideas and inventing new ways of doing things. They were looking for help to get more efficient so that they didn't need to hire anyone to take on the extra workload that was growing by the day. Their small business was growing consistently, and it was evident to me that she really needed to take on someone to help support the business growth, but she was really struggling to make the commitment and find someone. It soon became apparent that what was stopping her was that she was holding on to a limiting belief around running a successful business and being able to employee and manage staff. You see my client had watched her parents run a business, and in her teens watched how that company went bankrupt and impacted on her family. From then on her mum would always say to her, never run a business, get a good steady job, businesses only work for highly successful people who have lots of money to invest, not people like us. So my client, although very successful had been running this story through her mind and this belief about success had been keeping her stuck, unable to move forward for fear of not being able to sustain both the business and any employees she hired.

So rather than grow her company, even though her dream was to have a successful business, she limited herself and kept telling herself people like me don't run big businesses. I'm glad to report with a little help that my client was able to let this belief go and reinvent a new belief so she could go on to build a thriving successful printing business that now employs over forty people.

You see, it's easy not to be aware of old stories and beliefs that are running the show at an unconscious level, you just get so used to being and doing things in a certain way never questioning just accepting until that is something or someone forces you to look at things differently.

We are all capable of being and doing and creating a life exactly how we want it to be. We are all capable of RE-Inventing ourselves at any time. I want you to really believe that you are a born creator, and everything you imagine, positive or negative has the potential to be created just with that thought, especially when you align with it and take action on bringing it into your life.

However, all the right stuff we ask for, work for and create in our life is in vain, if we are unable to be fully open and willing to receive and accept it into our life, especially if we continue to hold on to old outdated beliefs, and stories we have about ourselves.

You are the sum total of what you believe you are, not what you say you are but what you think and feel at the deepest level. Remember what you believe about yourself is exactly what you will get, what you think at the deepest level of your unconscious mind will by played out in your reality no matter what you say or do.

Those beliefs, those old stories will find a way of sabotaging your success, so it is vital to change them and to allow an acceptance and capacity to receive all that you are worthy of, and you are worthy of having and being exactly what you desire.

Let's go back to the idea of acceptance. Remember I spoke of the importance of acceptance in the process of forgiveness? Well, we are back here again, and when it comes to re-inventing yourself, you must begin to learn to accept that you are worthy and deserving of the life you want to create and the dreams you would like to achieve. And that having all these things are good, relationships are good, money is good, and you are good. There is no point attempting to reinvent who you are, if you are going to carry all these old stories and beliefs you have about yourself that are negative.

Realise and accept that you can be anyone you want to be and to some extent, that's what you have been doing all along, you just haven't been doing it consciously or maybe choosing the most desirable version of you. Know that there is enough room for everyone, no matter what you desire, or how many other people are being and doing the things you want to be.

On some level the universe, God, Source, your consciousness or whatever you want to call it has everything under control and wants you to live the life you desire. So whatever you desire and believe yourself to be, you will create. After all, you came into this world with the potential to create yourself in any way you wish so why wouldn't it support and enable you to fulfill your TRUE potential! There is no scarcity, no matter what your ambitions or dreams are there is enough for everyone, more than sufficient and when you can accept that you create a space to actually embrace the creativity within to completely transform your life.

Your internal beliefs and the image you have of yourself is what determines, how much you can create, receive and keep in your life. It's time to start increasing that capacity for creation if you do not increase your capacity, you cannot have more, and you will eventually return to the same old beliefs you have about yourself.

Increasing your ability to create and reinvent yourself takes time, and involves practice and patience, you must be diligent otherwise old habits and beliefs will begin to return especially when you are unaware. Being committed to ditching your old beliefs and stories and being consciously aware of your own internal self-talk will enable you to increase that capacity and make changes that transform your life in the long run.

Chapter Five

"Whatever it is you're seeking won't come in the form you're expecting."

- Haruki Murakami

Step 5 - Ditch your expectations

I have so many friends and colleagues who are coaches and hypnotherapists and I have coached and mentored many of them over the years to help them build their business. Some are wonderful at growing their client base and their business and find it easy to meet new customers and take on new coaching contracts. Others really struggle. As I have observed the differences between those who seem to thrive naturally in their business or professional life and those who struggle what I notice more than anything is the level of expectations people place either on their self or others or the outcomes they hope to achieve.

Often setting intentions or goals and then not meeting these can impact on our self-belief, and when we have expectations of others, and they do not fulfill those expectations it can have a disastrous impact on how we live our life and our successes. When we set high expectations, and these are not met we can quickly fall into a victim mentality, blaming others or our circumstances for not being able to do or achieve the things we want.

When we set our expectations to have or be a certain thing or that someone else will fulfill some element of our life for us then we are attempting to control the outcomes of our life. But you cannot control anything at all, the only thing that is ever in your control are the thoughts and feelings you are experiencing in your mind. That's where we get it all wrong.

One of my most favourite clients said to me once I have put everything in place to guarantee that this will work so I expect it to work. Now, this client was talking about something that they could not possibly control the outcome of, no matter what things they had put in place to guarantee their success. The reason they couldn't guarantee the outcome was because this thing was dependant on another person, and guess what we cannot control others, we cannot control their thoughts, feelings or behaviours. We can attempt to influence them or in the case of my client create the necessary conditions that will help a person to be successful, but we cannot control what happens in reality. So, guess what? Yep, my client's expectations of their project were not met. When they came to work with me, they were in a place of huge disappointment, almost at a point of giving up.

I asked them why they put such high expectations on getting a result and they said because their business depended on it. Therein sits the problem with expectation. We cannot possibly control anything that is subject to influence that is outside of yourself. We can only control how we react or respond to life. We can either, set really high expectations and then let go of the outcome to the point where we do not allow the outcome of the event to affect us, or we can drop our expectations and give it everything we have got, without the need to have any expectations met. That way, it doesn't matter if something is successful or not, it's an experience that you learn from, and those learnings can then be put into something else so that you can have another more powerful experience based on what you have learned.

I have been guilty in the past of setting high expectations only to feel disappointed or let down when these expectations have not been met, either by myself or other people.

I am not saying not to be enthusiastic or confident in your life, what I am saying is to be realistic and lower your expectancy of what you expect or what others do for you. Do things without the need to control and let go of the outcome or expectations you have. That way you will never be disappointed, and you will always feel motivated to keep moving forward and doing things in life from a place of learning and growing.

I see all too often with my clients how they blame past relationship experiences or their current issues in that relationship for not meeting their expectations and I am always challenging them to be real about relationships. If they expect their relationships to always be full of roses and romance when the reality is that relationships take work. Only a very tiny percentage of the relationship will be filled with romantic gestures. By dropping expectations when the romance or whatever it is they expect to happen doesn't happen, they won't be disappointed and end yet another relationship because it didn't meet their expectations, or try and control the relationship.

Never give to others from a place of expectation. If you are going to give anything, whether that be your time, or something more tangible do it from a place of complete non-expectation. Give freely without looking for anything back.

My biggest awakening to this happened while running my business. After some years of working with people and helping them, I watched many of them become successful (often as a result of what I was giving away freely), and move on, leaving me behind. I became quite resentful and frustrated after a time, wondering what it was I was doing giving all this stuff away and no one being there to support me. I was at quite a low point in my life as my mother had not long passed away and was struggling with family relationships and the whole dynamic of grief not just for me but for my family too. It was during this time that I started to realise that although I thought I was giving for the sake of giving, somewhere at a deeper level, I was looking for something back. In the case of my family, after losing my mum, each time I gave, I was looking for their approval and acceptance. There was always some expectation of receiving something back, even if that was just a little attention!

I remember working with a client (who is now a very close friend) whom I would often give coaching sessions, materials, audios and a whole heap of my personal time to support her free of charge. Over time I began to feel resentment towards her for some of the success she was having, and I couldn't understand why I felt this way. After all, the very reason I was giving her all this additional support was because I wanted to help her be successful and I also give lots of stuff away and don't usually feel resentful. Again I was faced with this notion of expectation, and in the course of the two years that followed after my mother's death, I began spotting all the areas in my life at an alarming rate where I was giving with the expectation of getting something back. Not only was my awareness to this whole idea of giving starting to shift, but I also began seeing myself in a whole new light as well as seeing others in a whole new light. What I observed was that there were people who almost always give with no expectations of receiving anything back, they were often the ones who after gifting me something, whether it was their time, energy or support or something material I always left feeling lighter and more joyful. Even as I write this, I am receiving one of those types of gifts, as my cousin takes my daughter out for the day. I know this is done from a place of joy and that there is no expectation, I know this because of the joy and pleasure I feel from her being able to spend time with my six-year-old daughter, whom she doesn't get the chance to spend much time with. This is a gift given from a place of joy.

I have also become aware of another kind of giver; those who when they give, keep a mental record of what they did for you and expect something in return. It wasn't that they would always say it, it was more that I would just know that what they had done for me or the favour they had given, was done because there would be something I could do for them in return, either now, or in the future. In my line of work I meet many of these people and as my awareness of this grew I started to back away from these people as I realised that these were often the people who were the takers in life and never ever gave from a place of joy, just for the sake of giving.

After this awakening I began to look at all my relationships and reevaluate them, asking myself am I engaged in this relationship because of what I expect to get out of it or because of the joy of it. I spent the two years following the death of my mum completely reevaluating all my relationships both business and personal and reinventing all those relationships that were loaded with expectations on my part so I could transform them and give to them from a place of joy. To be honest, I had no idea how incredibly selfish I was, and how destructive that place of expectation can be and wish for the sake of both my parents I had to learn these lessons while they were both alive.

Give from a place of joy and for no other reason. Be a joyful giver, not someone who by giving looks for pay back or attempts to create win-win situations for themselves. I see this all the time in business. There are people I network with in business who are genuine givers, they give off their time, knowledge, wisdom, etc. freely and from a place of joy and the sheer love of lifting other people up. There are others who only share when you give them something, so when you offer them a gift of your knowledge or time, they feel compelled to give you something back. And there are also people who take, and take and take without ever giving, we all know these people and we soon get fed up with them. Now I choose to give freely of me and from a place of joy, I am doing it from a place of service with absolutely no expectation of getting anything back.

The gift of giving is not in what you get back but in the true fulfillment of watching someone being lifted by what you have given. Many people will say, "but I do give without expecting anything back!" and I am sure on some level like I did, they do, but I can almost always guarantee that when most people give, at a deeper unconscious level they are giving with the desire of expectancy.

If you really want to change the way you live I dare you to drop any expectations you have of yourself, other people and the work that you do and begin doing things just because you can and will do them. Focus on the pleasure of doing something rather than focusing on the outcome or on what you expect to get in recognition for doing that thing. By doing this, you will begin to notice that you only choose to do things that you really want to do; losing yourself in the process. When this happens you begin to live your life from a place of service, you connect with your purpose and your passion is fuelled, doing for the sake of doing becomes a natural, automatic way of doing things. No longer being focused on control or expectations you move into a place of flow, letting go and creating deeper joy and happiness in your life.

Chapter Six

"Appreciation is a wonderful thing. It makes what is excellent in others belong to us as well."

- Voltaire

Step 6 - Why gratitude on its own isn't enough

"Dance. Smile. Giggle. Marvel. TRUST. HOPE. LOVE. WISH. BELIEVE. Most of all, enjoy every moment of the journey, and appreciate where you are at this moment instead of always focusing on how far you have to go."

- Mandy Hale

You know one of the quickest ways I have found to start transforming my life and reinventing me is to begin by appreciating all that I already have. Yes, I know that might sound like a bit of a cliché, and no I am not talking about all the hype that you see out there on social media, posted on cute little memes or quotes about gratitude. To me, that's all wishy washy hype, to guilt us into remembering how lucky we are compared to others and to be grateful that "yep I have a roof over my head, I am grateful". I am talking about actually getting down and fully recognising and appreciating what it is that you have right there in front of you.

To me being grateful on its own isn't enough. There is so much information available out there on the importance of gratitude, and I certainly agree being grateful and being thankful for all that we have is so important, but it isn't enough, the missing ingredient from our lives is appreciation, and here is why I think this way.

The two words are almost always used to mean the same thing, yet they are different, and not only that these two words bring about different feelings and have different connotations. Both words while similar have a different emotional quality to them. Being thankful builds the foundation for appreciation, but we can be thankful for something without really appreciating it. We might live in a house, that is warm, has running water and comfortable furniture and be grateful or thankful we have that, but do we ever stop and fully appreciate these things? No, because while we are being grateful for this stuff we are busy thinking about all the things that we either don't have or want more of. So when you are grateful for that lovely house, you are simultaneously thinking, but I would like to have a better kitchen or live in a better neighbourhood or have a bigger house, or worse what everyone else has that you don't have! However, when we fully appreciate all that we have you are entirely focused on what's right there in front of you at that moment. You are consciously living in the present and are far more able to recognise the qualities of those things you have in your life.

When we fully appreciate something in our life, it causes us to reflect on how we feel, and when we appreciate all the gifts in our life, we feel good because we are savouring and enjoying the experience that those things we appreciate bring to us. The practice of appreciation, therefore, brings about a much deeper connection to the abundance we already have in our life, and we are not focussed on what we don't have but on what we do have. When we can recognise that connection then creating what we want becomes easy. What happens is when we are in a state of appreciation, is that whatever emotion that stir's in us this sentiment strengthens and the more we experience that feeling, the more we are able to bring these feelings into our life, thus increasing our levels of personal happiness. When we are happy our life transforms, we become more creative and creating new ways of being and doing becomes easy. Reinventing yourself and your life becomes effortless when you really appreciate who you are and all that you have and know that you can be and do even more with your life.

It's the feeling place within us that gives rise to our desires; we bring into our life exactly what we are feeling. If we are feeling gratitude but do not truly appreciate who we are or what we have then the emotion behind that lacks the depth of emotional quality that will provide the basis for what we want to bring into our life or the motivation to create even more. Whether that is relationships, money, business success, health or whatever it is that you want to have more abundantly. Being thankful or grateful isn't enough; you must feel the emotions that appreciation brings first before fully embodying the true nature of gratitude.

Believe it or not when we are appreciative of things rather than just feeling gratitude this alone can actually improve so many different aspects of our life. It can enhance our careers our relationships, it can also make people like us more. When you come from a place of appreciation you are far more likely to be effective at what you do, trust me taking things for granted and feeling obligated to be grateful for our life can often leave us feeling frustrated and lack the motivation to get out there and create what we really want to create. But when you really get down and fully appreciate things, motivation and joy come so much more naturally. It flows through you, as opposed to being forced out of you, from just feeling grateful or because you were told by your parents or teachers or your peers that you should be grateful for what you have.

When I first go into all the self-help and transformational stuff and people were talking about writing a gratitude journal and picking out one thing a day to feel grateful for and I really struggled with this idea. I thought that there must be something wrong with me, because I wasn't getting the same feelings that everyone else was describing when they were doing their daily gratitude practice. It left me feeling frustrated and thinking that maybe I was selfish. I remember one day sitting down and having a cup of coffee and as my mind wandered I began to be aware that I could feel the warmth of the cup in my hands. I started thinking how I really loved holding hot cups of coffee, especially when my hands were cold, and it was at that moment that I realised I was feeling grateful for this mug of coffee! I was overjoyed that I finally had something I could put in my gratitude journal that I felt genuinely grateful for, but I also realised as I reflected in my journal that it was what preceded my gratitude that gave rise to that thought of being thankful. The moment before gratitude kicked I was experiencing appreciating the mug of coffee and savouring the warmth of the mug in my hand and that emotion right there, which I later called contentment, that's what gave rise to those feelings of gratitude, not the thankfulness itself. From that one small thing, I completely changed my approach to my daily practice of gratitude and I focussed instead on appreciating what was going on in my life. No longer did I feel selfish because I couldn't find the feeling of gratitude inside when my husband emptied the dishwasher, after all, why should I feel grateful for something he should be taking his turn at! Now I could focus on appreciating that he does take his turn, sometimes even without being asked! And from there I am far more able to feel grateful for that small act of emptying a dishwasher.

You know feeling appreciative of what you have reduces feelings of jealousy and resentment. It can make memories of past experiences happier, and lets us enjoy more pleasant feelings, and helps us bounce back from stress far more quickly.

I help my clients with this all time, by helping them to shift their perspective on gratitude. Often I'm working with clients who want to make changes in their career and are fearful about changing jobs and doing something different. They will share with me how they feel guilty complaining about the work they do, especially when it's very well paid and has good hours, only because they think they should feel grateful as so many others don't have what they have. This is a common theme in many people's lives, and it keeps them feeling unhappy and disappointed in life. When we understand what happens when we begin to appreciate instead of being grateful, a huge shift takes place. It doesn't mean that my client will decide to stay in the dead end job or not look for something that will be more suited to them. What it will do however is help them to appreciate their situation in a new way making it easier for them to feel good about leaving it and moving on to something new and more beneficial for them. For example, my client Harry began to appreciate all the learning and experience that his job had given him, which lead to him feeling more joyful at the prospect of going into work every day and more motivated. He still wanted to find a new job because he felt stuck in his current role, but Harry stopped complaining and feeling guilty about something that previously he thought he should be grateful for. In my last session with Harry, he shared with me he had found a new job and told me that by appreciating his current role it made it much easier to go for interviews and secure a new post feeling in a more joyful and happy place. I do believe this to be true if we don't appreciate what we have, it shows, even if we are good at hiding it, somehow it will leak out of us through our body language, or our energy and people will notice. Any new potential employer or partner for that matter would be quick to pick up on that, whether consciously or unconsciously and would not be attracted to the person.

Lavish in the feelings of appreciating, all the yummy feelings that a relationship/s brought, savour the enjoyment of the money you have and how it makes you feel. Languish in the dream of how your business or career is going from strength to strength, completely indulge in the real feelings of being appreciative of these things. Appreciate all the great qualities you have as a person, focus on these and use these to help you reinvent you. We often forget to appreciate the person we are, what I really appreciate about me is that I am loving and fierce and brave, and often when I was at my lowest I forgot all about these qualities and didn't appreciate those parts of me. Now when I am reinventing any aspect of my life, I focus on these qualities and these adjectives about how I describe myself and use these to help me reinvent whatever it is I am reinventing about me. Maybe you can begin to see and feel now that the emotional quality of appreciation is far stronger than that of gratitude?

Gratitude isn't enough, but it's something that can and will grow when you sincerely appreciate all that you have. When you combine the two, you have a recipe for transforming any aspect of your life, all while feeling grateful without feeling obligated to do so.

Remember these wonderful words from Mahatma Gandhi, "The best way to find yourself is to lose yourself in the service of others."

Chapter Seven

"A girl should be two things: who and what she wants."

- Coco Chanel, The Gospel According to Coco Chanel

Step 7 - Get clear on who you really want to be

"When you are content to be simply yourself and don't compare or compete, everyone will respect you."

- Lao Tzu, Tao Te Ching

You cannot go about the business of reinventing yourself if you have no idea who you want to be or how you want your life to be. You need to start by getting clear on knowing who you are, what kind of person you are and what things you like about you and your life. Often it's the attributes and characteristics about ourselves that we value that we tend to hide or play down. When my eldest daughter was in primary school, she came home upset one day, and I asked her what made her unhappy. She told me that she had worked hard on a picture she had drawn and felt proud of her artistic ability, so she shared it with her teacher. Unfortunately, her teacher told her that "self-praise was no praise at all" and that she "shouldn't be so boastful of her abilities". This really knocked her confidence and caused her to want to hide her light away, it took a long time for her to bounce back from this experience and feel able to share her drawings and feel comfortable sharing with others the artistic and creative person she is. Often it's those parts of ourself that we are most proud of that we are taught to hide because people perceive it to be boastful when we talk about the things we are good at or aspects of our personality that we like. Yet, this constant hiding away of our light can result in us never feeling able to be ourselves. When my father passed away one of the last things he said to me was "just be you Avril" and yet in all the years I knew him I had this belief that he didn't like who I was so I tried to be everything other than "just me", ironic really! If you spend years trying to be who you think others want you to be you can lose sight of who you are and "just being you" can be challenging because you have forgotten who you are, or what you stand for. One of the gifts of reinventing yourself is that you can "just be you" or you can create a whole new you that is more aligned with who you want to be and the life you want to create.

This is your chance to bring all of the awesomeness to the fore and to start highlighting it. You get the opportunity to create a whole new version of you so start with the best bits, the bits you love about yourself and your life and then decide from there who you want to be. What's the point in putting in a pile of work and making changes in some areas of your life if you have no idea about the kind of person you are or who you want to become?

We experience such contradictions about who we should be, especially when we allow ourselves to be guided by the opinions or beliefs of others. On the one hand, it's not good to let too much of our light shine through and on the contrary we must hide all the darkness and put on a mask so nobody can see these darker sides of our personalities or nature. Being you is to be authentic, and one can only do this when both our light and dark are held in the balance.

One of the things I have always loved about me, is my fierceness and my ability to be brave, yet for years I played this down in favour of trying hard to be "nice" and "soft" or "gentle" and "loving", because I didn't believe people would accept me being fierce. Every one of us has degrees of polarities in our characters and personalities, the trouble is that more often than not we tend to focus on either one or the other. So while I love that I am gentle and loving, I continuously pushed into the background my brave, fierce side not fully embracing it and the power it added to my loving and kind nature. All too often we see our shadow sides as being negative, yet in life, there is always a balance. A Ying and a Yang. When we neglect aspects of ourselves for fear of what others might think or whether these parts of our being are either acceptable or unacceptable we can do this to the detriment of our growth and at the cost of living a happy, fulfilled and balanced life.

What I love most about the work that I do is helping others embrace their shadow self, there is something miraculous that happens when a client realises that for them to shine and be who they want to be both the light and dark sides of their nature must get an opportunity to be seen too. I witness this most powerfully when I work with clients longer term. Francis a beautiful lady I worked with for a year came to me because she had suffered from extreme anxiety since she was a child and had spent years seeing all sorts of therapists to try and rid herself of this anxiety. We only worked on the anxiety specifically for two sessions together. In one of the sessions we focussed on bringing the anxiety part of her into balance and in harmony with all the other parts of her personality and the transformation was amazing. Yes at this point she was her anxiety, but she was also much, much more than this. Once she found a way to embrace and welcome that part of her personality a shift began to happen, very soon her anxiety levels began to drop to a point where she was no longer having her episodes of anxiety attacks. Working with her I helped her to find a way to work with that anxiety positively and to enhance the person she wanted to become. Twelve months on this lovely lady was able to engage in her life entirely and went on to change her career and do something she had always wished she'd had the confidence to do in her early twenties. She now has Masters Degree in Psychology and is working with a children's charity to help children with childhood anxiety.

We are not one-dimensional beings, we are multidimensional, there is always more than one side to who we are. A teacher I greatly admire and respect calls this the "mandala self" and suggests that we are not, merely the sum total of the beliefs and opinions that others have of us, or that you have of yourself. We are all of these things and much, much more, and to ignore the many different aspects of our being and only fixate on what's appealing to us and to others is to do so at the cost of our personal well-being and growth. By being fixed to our beliefs, opinions and even values we become stuck and inflexible, we close off the opportunity to transform and grow. We then find it difficult to see different perspectives and in some extremes be respectful or even tolerate others beliefs or ways of living. So many of the people I work with are living life in this way, and will say to me "but that's just who I am". Or "This is what I believe, and if someone doesn't fit into that well I can't change, and I can't possibly share a life with them". It's such a limited way of being, yet when we work together and delve deeper into this idea that they are much, much more than what they believe themselves to be; that position they were fixated on begins to loosen. As soon as this happens they open to the possibility that they are multidimensional and to thrive all parts of their being must be allowed to shine, both their light and their darkness.

As well as knowing who you are and who you want to be you need to make sure that your dreams and vision for your future completely support the person you are creating and aligns with you. If you are reinventing you and creating a whole new persona, then do all those values and beliefs you hold still ring true for the new you? If there is a mismatch, I can pretty much guarantee you that reinventing you will be challenging. I have had personal experience of this off and on throughout the years. When my dreams are out of sync with the person, I want to be and when my values don't match up with how I want to live my life then I have difficulty making my dreams happen. Or when I do achieve what I set out to create I do not have the fulfillment or happiness that I thought that these dreams would bring to me.

Not so long ago I collaborated on a project, and whilst the project was enjoyable and the work interesting as time wore on I increasingly became more and more unhappy. There was nothing specifically wrong, it just felt at times that something wasn't clicking and I constantly had a niggling feeling that what I was doing didn't sit right with me. I couldn't understand this because this project was something I had always wanted to do and something I was passionate about. However when I checked in with myself, and my values and aligned them to the collaboration that I was involved in I very quickly realised the problem. The project was a great idea, but how it was coming together and my role in it didn't match with the fully integrated and balanced me. I realised when I began the project I wasn't bringing all parts of who I was to the table. I was holding aspects of my multidimensional self back for fear of being rejected and when these other parts of me started trying to get my attention and wanting to be seen I soon became uncomfortable. That feeling I had, that little nagging that went on inside was these parts of me that I was hiding away attempting to get my attention. When I realised this and checked in to see if I felt comfortable in the project being me. I found that much to my disappointment all of me was not what this project required, I took the decision as soon as I recognised this to walk away from what could have been a very successful collaboration.

It's so important to trust your feelings. That little voice that we all call intuition or gut feel is usually calling you to pay attention to your shadow self, often to parts of you that are being hidden. Your intuition will not explain what the problem is, that's up to you to discover for yourself. However, if you are present and fully aware, like me you can take the necessary action to check in with yourself and make whatever adjustments you need to get you back on the path to your dreams, your passion or your call in life.

Chapter Eight

"The future depends on what you do today."

- Mahatma Gandhi

Step 8 - Stop waiting on the universe to deliver and take action

"Action may not always bring happiness, but there is no happiness without action."

- William James

If you really want to reinvent you and transform your life, then you really must get clear on your vision and take action to make it happen. Without action, the vision you have for your life and how you want to live your life will never happen. Whether it's better health, more money, a new job, a new relationship, etc... whatever it may be, you must first be clear in your heart and mind about where it is you would like to go. That means aligning your conscious mind with your unconscious mind and ensuring that any old limiting beliefs that have been hidden from view are cleared to enable you to move forward.

Get a daily routine together, create good habits of the mind and focus on the small things. Give yourself mini projects to work on rather than big goals; sometimes the word goal can put pressure on us to achieve something big. When I work with my coaching clients I encourage them to change their goals to projects, and within the projects there are little steps that they take to bring that project to fruition. Never give yourself a deadline for achieving the big vision, only give deadlines to the little projects you are working on that will move you closer towards your big dream and the vision you have for your life.

Think of yourself as a pilot of an aeroplane. The destination the pilot is flying towards is just like the vision or the dream you have for your life. The pilot can never see the end goal when they sit down in the pilot seat, but they do know where they are going, they have an eye on the big picture, but their focus is on the steps that they need to take to get there. All their focus is on the minor adjustments that need to be made along the way for them to reach their final destination. Like the pilot you know where you want to end up but can't always see the end result until there and in most cases what you want will invariably evolve so there is never a final outcome or destination. It's more a tweaking or readjustment of your vision, constantly realigning to the person and life you are creating, moment, by moment. Once the aeroplane is in that sky the pilot has to rely on the navigation screen in the cockpit, the only view outside is the sky. Sometimes they may get a glimpse of life below or have an idea of what the destination looks like because they have been somewhere similar before. Pilots make tiny adjustments along the way to their final destination, sometimes they have to go off course in order steer back in the right direction and so it is like that with our dreams, and if we never get ourselves in the pilot seat we will never take off. You have to be in that seat to notice the adjustments that are required to steer you towards your dream.

Just like the pilot heading for their destination, we will never have an entirely clear view of how our ideas will end up looking or how to get there. Sometimes you get glimpses of what it might end up looking like but until you sit in the pilot seat and start navigating in the direction of your dreams you really won't know what you need to do to get there or what's involved. Now that may seem a bit far reached, but I want you to think back on your life and notice how those things you set out to achieve were most likely never met in their entirety, more likely those dreams or goals you had evolved and changed along the way. But you have got to get in the driver's seat and start taking action!

Taking action is a vital ingredient, I have worked with so many people of over the years that complain and bemoan that they have been putting their desires and dreams out to the universe and yet it still never happens. You must take action to move towards your dreams no matter how small those steps are; in fact, no step is too small. Sitting on the couch, or meditating on it just isn't going to bring it into your reality, you must be clear on this.

We were born to create, and no matter what you think there is nobody but you that can make change happen. No secret ingredient, or auspicious alignment of the stars or universe that will come along and bring to you all that you desire. You are the only one responsible for this, and the moment you start taking the action you will begin to create opportunities to bring more into your life. Sitting back and sending an intention out into the universe without any action just won't work. Take a look around at those people who you believe are living their dreams; ask yourself are they just sitting back expecting the universe to deliver everything they desire to them on their lap? I bet your answer is no, and I can guarantee that they are doing something purposeful each and every day that is propelling them forward towards their dreams, creating and reinventing their life in each and every moment, even if you don't notice it or know what it is they are doing.

I really want you to get this, the only thing that is going to enable you to reinvent you and transform your life is you and the action you take. The only thing that is keeping you stuck is you and the thoughts you are thinking and the beliefs you are buying into. That universe, that is so often mentioned in self-help and some spiritual books is your mind. This is what everyone seems to miss and is the actual secret. People are missing the point all the time, and allowing themselves to get caught up in some mystical idea that the universe has their back and if they just put it out there and think positively enough it will come to them. Well, I have been putting it out there for years and the only universe that has my back are my own thoughts, my own beliefs and my own values all of which reside in my own mind. Never in my entire 49 years have I put something out to the universe, and it has arrived without any will or intent or action that has not come from me.

People are always asking me how do I just seem to make a decision and hey presto it happens. My response to that is this: "Yes I do get what I want, but I take action to make it happen, it doesn't just arrive all gift wrapped from the universe. Every single tiny little thing that I have created in my life up until this point both positive and negative has been as a result of me taking inspired action on some level to create it and to make it happen".

I pay close attention to my inner voice (intuition) when it calls me to listen. I listen and respond accordingly, I never sit there and just wait and see, or wait till it feels right or wait for a sign. I go out there and look for what it is that I need to do next, and then act on anything that calls me to action.

Whenyou act and start reinventing your life more opportunities, coincidences and serendipity will begin to appear to you, not because of the universe outside of you but because of the universe of your mind. You are making changes to your thoughts, your beliefs and your attitudes and of course, things are going to change. With each change you make on the inside the world outside can and will change. You begin to learn to live life according to your will not according to the will of the universe or the last horoscope or angel card reading you had.

And when this happens you know you are moving in the right direction, so you must always take action on them, and if something comes to you more than twice, you really do need to pay attention and listen as the universe is trying to get your attention!

Stop sitting on the couch and sending orders to the universe, to God or source or whatever you want to call it. Focus on your mind, get flexible change your thoughts, your beliefs and get aligned with who you want to be and go out there take action and start reinventing your life today.

About The Author

Avril is an inspirational teacher and coach and has been helping people transform both their lives and career for over 20 years. Working initially in the Financial services sector building her career in HR and Learning and Development where she gained valuable career capital and insight before setting up and running her own business in 2008.

Avril teaches Hypnotherapy & Coaching and transformational retreats, as well as her "Reinvent You" retreat experiences around the world and helps small business owners transform their businesses as well as helping everyday people like you and me reinvent their lives and careers.

Avril lives in Scotland and splits her time working between Edinburgh and Fife, she is married to Alan and has two daughters, Alison age 24 and Ara age 6. Avril is passionate about living life to the full, and believes that to do this one must keep everything simple and uncomplicated, especially our thinking. She has two little dogs that keep her company while working and writing in Fife.

Next steps with Avril @ www.avrilgill.com

"You never change things by fighting the existing reality. To change something, build a new model that makes the existing model obsolete." -R. Buckminster Fuller"

"Most Coaches have a program to follow. They use exercises and tweak things to improve your life and business. Almost like when an artist comes along and adds a little paint here or there to enhance the photo.

Me, well I have no particular exercises or colour enhancers, because you become a blank canvas, and you are the material. My coaching is reimagining and reinventing you and working with what you want to bring to the canvas and create."

Avril Gill @ www.avrilgill.com

Printed in Great Britain
by Amazon

33704610R00046